Table of Contents

How to add another owner to LLC

INTRODUCTION

A limited liability company (LLC) is a business structure in the U.S. that protects its owners from personal responsibility for its debts or liabilities. Limited liability companies are hybrid entities that combine the characteristics of a corporation with those of a partnership or sole proprietorship.

While the limited liability feature is similar to that of a corporation, the availability of flow-through taxation to the members of an LLC is a feature of a partnership rather than an LLC.

Limited liability companies are permitted under state statutes, and the regulations governing them vary from state to state. LLC owners are generally called members.

Many states don't restrict ownership, meaning anyone can be a member including individuals, corporations, foreigners, foreign entities, and even other LLCs. Some entities, though, cannot form LLCs, including banks and insurance companies.

DIFFERENT TYPES OF LLC

A limited liability company (LLC) is a legal business entity structure that offers owners personal risk protection and a bevy of flexible tax options. This entity type is a reliable choice for new business owners and startups because it limits the risk of an owner's personal assets being seized to pay the debts and obligations of the company.

Additionally, owners can elect a pass-through tax status. That means any business profits bypass taxation at the corporate level and are assessed entirely on an owner's personal income tax return. This avoids the double taxation issue common with corporations that choose C corporation (C-corp) tax status.

LLCs are easy to organize and maintain so long as you register the business with the state, pay the renewal fees, and follow the required formalities. Still, there are many facets to LLCs, and not all of them are apparent at first glance. LLCs come in a variety of different types, which can vary from state to state. Knowing about these LLC types and where they are available can help you decide which one is right for your business.

UNDERSTANDING DIFFERENT TYPES OF LLCS

You might be thinking that LLCs seem straightforward. The good news is they pretty much are! However, the many intricacies of business have necessitated the creation of different types of LLCs over time.

LLCs are governed by the states in which they are organized. Organizing an LLC means you've registered the business with the state's governmental business authority (typically, a secretary of state). This process includes drafting an operating agreement between the owners and filing articles of organization with the state. Once organized, the LLC is created, and the government will view it as a separate legal entity from its owner. This means your personal assets are protected if the LLC has debts or faces a lawsuit.

A critical point in organizing your company will be choosing what kind of LLC your business will be. For an important decision like this, you will need to research what types of LLC are offered in the state where you plan to organize. Here are a few types of LLCs that are worth being aware of; they are each described in detail further below:

- Single-member LLCs
- Multiple-member LLCs
- Member-managed LLCs
- Manager-managed LLCs
- Professional limited liability companies (PLLCs)
- Family limited partnerships
- L3C companies
- Series LLCs (only available in Delaware, Nevada, Iowa, Illinois, Tennessee, Oklahoma, Utah, and Texas)
- Restricted LLCs (only available in Nevada)
- Anonymous LLCs (only available in New Mexico)

Note that these types are not exclusive and can often apply to the same LLC. Sometimes, a manager-managed LLC will also be owned by single-member, and vice versa. It's worth checking with your state to see which structure best fits your business.

Single-Member LLCs

Single-member LLCs are recognized in every state and are the most common type of LLC. Here, the word "member" is a stand-in for "owner." Single-member LLCs have an individual owner. The Internal Revenue Service (IRS) treats them as sole proprietorships for tax purposes.

Multiple-Member LLCs

As you might've guessed, multiple-member LLCs are simply LLCs with multiple owners. Multiple-member LLCs are structured similarly to general partnerships. All owners are responsible for the debts and obligations of the company, but their personal assets are still secure. Members each have the option to decide how they want to pay taxes on their share of the business's profits.

Member-Managed LLCs

This is an LLC that the members, or owners, of the company manage. The decision of whether to be member-managed or manager-managed is made when the LLC organizes. Of the two, member-managed LLCs are more common in the United States.

Manager-Managed LLCs

In member-managed LLCs, the members decide on managers and ascribe responsibilities and duties. Managers are named in the operating agreement, which the owners then sign. Owners can be managers. Any owners who aren't also managers are not required to partake in the management of the business if they do not wish to.

PLLCs

These are LLCs for industries that require professional licensure. They are a typical structure for accountants, doctors, and lawyers. PLLCs ensure that owners are not legally responsible for the malpractice of other owners.

Requirements for PLLCs can be different from state to state. If you're an owner in an industry requiring state licensure, it's best to consult your state's governmental business authority to determine what's needed.

L3C Companies

L3Cs are for-profit entities formed for humanitarian efforts. L3Cs are often chosen for their pass-through taxation and their similarity to non-profits.

Series LLCs

Series LLCs take the company's debts and obligations and attribute them to smaller units within the LLC, called series. These units can include owners, managers, and other company assets.

Suppose that a series LLC has designated its debts and obligations to you, an owner of the company. In this circumstance, these debts and obligations are your responsibility and can be enforced if commitments are not met. It can often be a big responsibility for designated units of a series LLC.

This type of LLC is currently only available in Delaware, Iowa, Illinois, Nevada, Oklahoma, Tennessee, Texas, and Utah.

Restricted LLCs

Restricted LLCs work a little differently for business owners than more traditional formats. That's because owners have a 10-year waiting period from organizing before they can start receiving business distributions.

Restricted LLCs are only available in Nevada.

Anonymous LLCs

Anonymous LLCs are for owners that want to keep their company's details private. Here, information access is restricted, so the public cannot obtain details on ownership and structure.

Anonymous LLCs are currently only available in New Mexico.

BENEFITS OF AN LLC

Structuring your business as an LLC offers a number of advantages.

Limited liability

Members aren't personally liable for actions of the company. This means the members' personal assets — homes, cars, bank accounts, investments — are protected from creditors seeking to collect from the business. This protection stays in as you run your business on the up-and-up and keep business and personal financials separate.

Pass-through federal taxation on profits

Unless it opts otherwise, an LLC is a pass-through entity, meaning its profits go directly to its members without being taxed by the government on the company level. Instead, members pay tax on the profits on their own federal income tax returns.

This makes filing taxes easier than if your business were taxed on the corporate level.

If your business loses money, you and other members can shoulder the hit on your own tax returns and lower your tax burdens.

Management flexibility

Members can manage an LLC, which allows all owners to share in the business's day-to-day decision-making.

Alternatively professional managers, who can be either members or outsiders, can manage the business. This is helpful if members want to hire people who are more experienced running a business.

In many states, an LLC is member-managed by default unless explicitly stated otherwise in filings with the secretary of state or the equivalent agency.

Easy startup and upkeep

Initial paperwork and fees for an LLC are relatively light, though there is wide variation in what states charge in fees and taxes. The process is simple enough for owners to handle without special expertise, though it's a good idea to consult a lawyer or an accountant for help. Ongoing requirements usually come on an annual basis.

DISADVANTAGES OF AN LLC

Before registering your business as an LLC, consider these possible drawbacks.

Limited liability has limits

A judge can rule that your LLC structure doesn't protect your personal assets. The action is called "piercing the corporate veil," and you can be at risk if, for example, you don't clearly separate business transactions from personal transactions or if you run the business fraudulently in ways that caused losses for others.

Self-employment tax

The IRS considers LLCs as partnerships for tax purposes, unless members opt to be taxed as a corporation.

If your LLC is taxed as a partnership, the government considers members who work for the business to be self-employed. This means those members are personally responsible for paying Social Security and Medicare taxes, which are collectively known as self-employment tax, based on the business's total net earnings.

If your LLC files forms with the IRS to be taxed as an S corporation, you and other owners who work for the company pay Social Security and Medicare taxes only on your actual compensation rather than on all the company's pretax profits.

Consequences of member turnover

In many states, if a member leaves the company, goes bankrupt or dies, the LLC must be dissolved and the remaining members are responsible for all remaining legal and financial obligations necessary to terminate the business. These members can still do business, of course; they'll just have to start a whole new LLC from scratch.

DIFFERENCE BETWEEN LLC AND INC.

Business names often have abbreviations after them, including LLC and inc. Find out what these abbreviations mean and how an LLC is different from a corporation.

You may have noticed that business names often end with an abbreviation such as LLC or inc. But what do those abbreviations mean? What is the difference between LLC and inc.? In fact, what is an LLC? The letters may seem confusing, but LLC and inc. are abbreviations for different kinds of business entities.

"LLC" stands for limited liability company. The abbreviations "inc." and "corp." indicate that a business is a corporation.

Corporations issue shares of stock to their owners, who are called shareholders. Corporate shares are easy to transfer from one owner to another, and therefore a corporation can be a good choice for a business that anticipates having outside investors or making a public stock offering.

The owners of an LLC are called "members," and instead of shares, each member owns a designated percentage of the company, sometimes called a "membership interest."

Membership in an LLC may be more difficult to transfer than shares in a corporation. An LLC's operating agreement will typically specify whether and how membership interests can be transferred.

In some states, if a member leaves an LLC and the operating agreement does not specify otherwise, the LLC must be dissolved.

TAXES

One of the biggest differences between corporations and LLCs is the way they are taxed. Let's examine how taxation for each business structure works.

LLC Taxes

An LLC is taxed as a pass-through entity by default. This means that the profits of the business are "passed through" to the owners (called members). Profits and losses are reported on the individual tax returns for the owners, and not at the business level. As a result, filing taxes is often simpler for owners of an LLC. Any losses or operating costs of the business can be deducted on personal tax returns, which can help offset other income.

The rate at which an LLC is taxed depends on the total income of the owner, as it does when you file as a sole proprietor. Owners of an LLC may also be required to pay self-employment taxes. Some states require LLCs to pay a franchise tax. This is a tax issued by the state for the privilege of doing business in that state. Franchise taxes are usually paid annually and vary from state to state.

What happens if you do not pay your taxes? Failing to pay on time or at all could result in penalties and even the involuntary dissolution of your business.

Luckily, incorporating as an LLC provides entrepreneurs with flexibility. An LLC may elect to be taxed as

Corporation or an C Corporation. While it is an uncommon choice, filing an LLC as a C Corp tax designation does make financial sense for some businesses.

Corporation Taxes

Corporations are taxed as a separate legal entity, which can earn its own income. Corporations are responsible for paying tax on their profits, (corporate tax), and tax on dividends the entity distributes to its shareholders. Since dividends are not tax deductible (like salaries and bonuses), dividends are taxed twice. This is referred to as double taxation. This is not an issue for smaller corporations where only the owners work for the corporation. Instead, owners receive tax deductible salaries and bonuses.

While double taxation is seen as a disadvantage for businesses choosing to file as a corporation, this additional tax responsibility can often be offset by federal deductions that are only available to corporations.

For example, a corporation may deduct all its business expenses. These can include advertising costs and operating expenses as well as certain employee fringe benefits such as medical and retirement plans. These deductions all add up to substantial savings over time for the business.

As of 2018, corporations pay a flat tax of 21% on their profits, which is lower than the top five individual tax rates. While this is largely offset by double taxation, any income the corporation chooses to retain at the end of the year will be taxed only once at the new 21% rate. This allows the owners of the corporation to save on taxes by investing some profits back into the business.

Keep in mind if a corporation has fewer than 100

shareholders, it can file an S Corporation election. This is a tax status that allows a business to be treated as a pass-through entity much like an LLC. This may be a good option for businesses who want to be taxed like an LLC, but also want some of the additional formalities a corporation provides. The S Corporation designation does allow flow-through taxation (no corporate tax), but there are certain requirements to qualify as an S Corp that may limit its utility to a business.

S Corporation Taxes

If a business qualifies as an S Corporation, the tax difference between an LLC and S Corp is a bit more nuanced. Both an LLC and an S Corp has flow-through taxation (no double taxation). Keep in mind that an LLC's distribution of profits are subject to an employment tax, whereas an S Corp's dividends are not.

BUSINESS OWNERSHIP

Ownership is another important aspect to keep in consideration when deciding between whether to form an LLC and a corporation. The structure of ownership in each entity is very different, and each has a clear purpose which makes choosing the right entity for your business a bit easier.

A corporation can issue shares of stock and sell percentages of the business to its owners, which are called shareholders. These shareholders can transfer shares, purchasing more stock to own a larger percentage of the company, or selling off stock to own less. If your business is one that wants to attract outside investors, a corporation may be the best entity for it. A corporation also exists in perpetuity separate from the owners, meaning that a corporation remains in existence even when an owner leaves or divests from the company.

A Limited Liability Company (LLC) has the freedom to distribute its ownership stake to its members without regard to a member's financial contribution to the LLC. Let's use the example where a member of the LLC may not have invested as much capital as another member. An LLC's operating agreement could specify that all members receive an equal share of the profits anyway. This creates additional flexibility when establishing the ownership of the business.

An LLC can also be owned by foreign individuals, other corporations, or any kind of trust. This may make it the right choice for businesses in certain circumstances where these factors are important.

An LLC's operating agreement also outlines the details about how membership interest can be transferred between its members, if at all, and what happens when a member leaves the LLC. By default, if not defined in the operating agreement, when a member leaves the LLC it must be dissolved.

MANAGEMENT

An LLC has a flexible management structure. The entity can be managed by its members or a group of managers, and any member may act as the LLC's manager. The LLC may also elect to have no distinction between an owner and a manager of the business. Due to its flexible nature, LLC management is less formal which may make it an ideal entity for some entrepreneurs.

What is the difference between "manager-managed" and "member-managed" LLCs? In a member-managed LLC, the owners themselves oversee running the day to day operations, while a manager-managed LLC generally has investors that sit on the side lines, and don't have any other active role in the business.

A corporation's management structure is much stricter. A corporation must have a formal structure with a Board of Directors handling the management responsibilities of generating profits for the shareholders. Corporate officers are assigned to handle the day-to-day operations of the business. The shareholders are considered owners of the corporation but remain separate from business decisions and daily operations of the corporation (except for approval of major corporate decisions).

However, shareholders retain the power to elect directors, and individual shareholders can be elected as a director or appointed as an officer. The individual rules of any corporation are dictated by its corporate bylaws, which is a detailed set of rules adopted by the Board of Directors after the corporation is formed.

FORMAL
REQUIREMENTS

Both corporations and LLCs are required to fulfill maintenance and/or reporting requirements set by the state where their entity has been formed. This keeps the business in good standing and maintains the limited liability protection acquired by incorporation. While every state has its own rules and regulations that govern both corporations and LLCs, corporations generally have more annual requirements than LLCs.

Corporations are required to hold an annual shareholder meeting each year. These details are documented, along with any discussions, as notes called corporate minutes. A corporation is generally required to file an annual report, too. This helps keep the business' information current with the Secretary of State. Any actions or changes in the business will require a corporate resolution to be voted on at a meeting with the board of directors.

LLCs, on the other hand, have fewer record keeping requirements than their corporation counterparts. For example, an LLC is not required to keep minutes, hold annual meetings, or have a board of directors. While some states still require LLCs to file annual reports, others do not. Check in with your local Secretary of State to determine which requirements are applicable to your LLC entity.

LEGAL DISCREPANCIES

Both LLCs and corporations provide benefits to its owners when it comes to legal protections, although there are differences between the two and how they are seen by the court system.

Corporations have been in existence since the start of U.S. history. Because of this, a corporation as an entity has matured and developed to the point where the laws have become uniform. United States courts have centuries of law history cases to help resolve disputes and issues related to corporations. This creates significant legal stability for corporations.

Limited Liability Companies are still considered to be relatively "new." Their entity was first recognized in the 1970s as the offspring of both the corporate and sole proprietorship/partnership form. Due to this dual nature, an LLC takes on the characteristics of both legal entities. However, as a result of being a "new" legal entity and having characteristics of both a corporation and partnership, states differ in their treatment of LLCs.

While most states have similar LLC laws, there are differences that may lead a business to choose to become an LLC in one state and a corporation in another. In time, LLC laws will become more uniform throughout the

United States. For most businesses, these discrepancies between LLC laws should not be a factor, but the discrepancies may be the deciding factor for a few.

ARTICLES OF ORGANIZATION

As you no doubt know already, to form an LLC, members file articles of organization—also called a certificate of formation or a certificate of organization—with the state's business filing office.

This is usually the Secretary of State's office, but it can vary. For example, in Maryland, the office that regulates businesses is called the State Department of Assessments and Taxation, while in Arizona, it is called the Arizona Corporation Commission.

The articles of organization is a document that sets out basic information about the business. Typically, all you need to provide is:

- the name and principal address of the LLC
- the name and address of the registered agent
- information about the owners, managers, and officers
- a description of the business
- signature or signatures of the organizer or organizers of the LLC and the manager or managers, if named

Because this information varies by state, always check with your state's filing office for your state's specific requirements. Once the document is approved, the LLC is legally created and registered as a new entity.

LLC ARTICLES OF ORGANIZATION

To start an LLC, you'll need to create articles of organization. This simple document lays out basic information about your LLC—like the name of your company and the purpose of your business. File it with the appropriate state office to make your LLC an official entity.

States vary in how they refer to the document and the office where you will file it. This guide covers what LLC articles of organization are, how to file them, and important state information you should know to make your LLC official.

Articles of organization, sometimes known as a certificate of organization or certificate of formation, is an official document that outlines basic details about your company. You must file this document with your state in order to officially establish a business as an LLC. You can think of them as birth certificates for your company.

Depending on your Secretary of State's office, it can take a few business days or up to several weeks to get a response, but most states offer an expedited option. Once these articles are approved and filed, the LLC becomes a legal business entity.

The Secretary of State will review the articles of

organization, but there is a chance they may reject them. When they are not approved, it is usually due to issues with the LLC's suggested name, filing the wrong entity, or not following state-specific guidelines for filing.

You can usually fix incorrect articles of organization and resubmit them by filing an article of amendment, which details the specific changes to the information included in your article of organization.

PURPOSE

The purpose of articles of organization is to establish details such as the powers, duties, and obligations of your LLC at a state level.

Each state has different requirements for what's needed, but the most common information includes:

- LLC name
- Description/purpose of the LLC
- LLC's address
- Name and address of the registered (or statutory) agent
- Information about the LLC members, managers, and officers
- The date you'll start the LLC

Do you need articles of organization for an LLC?

Yes. If you are planning to start an LLC, you are required to file an article of organization with the Secretary of State and pay a filing fee—no matter what state you reside in.

ARTICLES OF INCORPORATION VS. ARTICLES OF ORGANIZATION

Articles of organization and articles of incorporation often get used interchangeably. Although they have the same purpose of outlining the details of your business, there is one key difference.

Articles of organization are for businesses interested in forming an LLC.

Articles of incorporation are for businesses interested in forming a corporation.

However, some states may use one name for all business structures, or a different name. Make sure to check your state's rules to see if there are specific filing guidelines for separate business entities.

HOW TO FILE ARTICLES OF ORGANIZATION

To begin filing LLC articles of organization, you'll need to have information about your company on hand. Here is a basic breakdown of how to file articles of organization for your LLC.

Visit your Secretary of State website

Your Secretary of State's website should outline the requirements for filing articles of organization. Information to look for includes:

- LLC articles of organization form
- Whether or not you can file the form online
- The filing cost. Depending on the state, the price is typically between $50 and $150, but it could be much higher depending on your state.
- Any follow-up instructions

Gather your information

Before filing, make sure to gather all of the information you'll need to file. Here is a list of some of the important information that most states will require you to have:

- LLC name: You need to have a name for your

LLC. It's important that you check your state's business website to ensure the business name you want isn't already taken.

- LLC address: You'll need to provide the physical address of your LLC. In some states, an address may be required rather than a P.O. box. Your Secretary of State's website will help you understand address requirements for your state.
- Start date: You'll need to provide a start date. This is typically the day you file the articles of organization or the date your article or organization is approved. Your state will give direction on any specific start date requirements if there are any.
- Registered agent: A registered agent is someone you designate to receive the legal paperwork for your business, like service of process notices, government correspondence, and compliance-related documents. You'll need to provide the name and address of your registered agent on your form.
- Registered agent: a person you designate to receive the legal paperwork for your business.

Prepare additional information

Before you can complete your LLC's articles of organization application, your state will require you to submit additional information, such as operational and organizational details. Here are some examples of what your state may ask you:

- LLC purpose: Some states may want you to state the purpose of your LLC. For example, some

LLCs must enter a single professional purpose when filing, like accounting services or law practice.

- LLC manager: Will a manager or group of members manage the LLC? This is something you need to be prepared to answer. Member-managed LLCs usually have fewer members and are involved in the day-to-day operations. Manager-managed LLCs sometimes have a larger number of members who aren't involved in day-to-day management.
- Members: In some states, you need to provide information about the initial members of the LLC, such as addresses and names. Additionally, there is no max amount of members to include in your list.

Submit the form

Once you provide the necessary information, you'll need to submit your LLC articles of organization for approval. Depending on how your state lets you file, you can either send your paperwork in the mail with a check payment or file it electronically.

Tip: Double-check and make sure your articles of organization are signed—it must be done by the authorized representative of the LLC.

If required: Publish a notice

Arizona, Nebraska, and New York require LLCs to publish a notice of formation in their local newspaper. Each state may have different publishing requirements, but your notice should typically include:

- Your LLC's name

- What county your LLC is located in and its address
- The LLC's purpose
- The name of the LLC's registered agent
- The date of your file was approved

Make sure to check your state's publishing guidelines, as there may be an additional fee or specific requirements you'll need to meet.

STEPS TO TAKE AFTER FILING

After you file your LLC articles of organization and they've been approved, there are some other documents and actions you should consider. Here are five things you'll want to make sure you complete after filing:

Get an EIN

An EIN, or an employer identification number, is a nine-digit number given to a company by the IRS for purposes of identification. An EIN is also known as a federal employer identification number or a federal tax identification number.

EINs are essentially Social Security numbers for your business and are usually required to open a business banking account, obtain a business license, or file a business tax return.

Create an LLC operating agreement

To ensure your LLC operates smoothly, you need to create an operating agreement. This agreement outlines your business' functional and financial decisions including regulations, rules, and provisions. Operating agreements are important because they protect your business against personal and financial liabilities, trade secret sharing, and conflicts of interest.

The operating agreement should outline things like member responsibilities and roles, member titles, and contributions.

Open a bank account

Now that you have an LLC designation, you can open an LLC bank account. Utilizing a business account for your LLC is more manageable than using your personal one because all your business expenses can be found in one place. It's important to maintain a separation between your personal and business finances to protect your personal assets from liability.

Your business accounts should only be used for business purposes so you can properly check your business's financial records.

Opening a bank account for your LLC is also the first step toward establishing business credit.

Business checking account: an account separate from your personal account that allows you to accept credit card payments from clients and customers.

Get a business license

Depending on the type of business you are opening and your state's regulations, you may need a business license. This license will ensure you comply with all state, county, and local laws. You'll need to reach out to your city's licensing authority to obtain an application, or it may also be available online.

File an annual report

In many states, you must file an annual report for your LLC. Filing this report keeps your company compliant with all state regulations and in good standing to preserve your limited liability protection and other benefits.

Note: If you do business in more than one state, you may be required to file an annual report in each state.

FILING ARTICLES OF ORGANIZATION BY STATE

While most states require similar information when filing articles of organization, every state has its own filing requirements and different fees, processing times, and ways to submit. Here is some key state information to know before filing.

Alabama: Articles of organization, referred to as a certificate of formation in Alabama, must be filed with the Alabama Secretary of State. There is a $200 formation filing fee that you can pay by check, money order, or credit card payment. You must mail two copies of the completed form and must include your name reservation certificate.

Alaska: Articles of organization in Alaska must be filed with the State of Alaska Corporations Section. There is a $250 filing fee, and it can take 10 to 15 days to process the application.

Arizona: Articles of organization in Arizona must be filed with the Arizona Corporate Commission. There is a $50 filing fee, and it can take 13 to 15 days to process the application. If you'd like to expedite the processing time, there will be an additional $35 fee. After your articles are approved, you'll be required to publish a notice in the newspaper.

Arkansas: A certificate of organization in Arkansas must be filed with the Arkansas Secretary of State. There is a $50 paper fee when mailing in the form, or you can fill out the online form for a $45 fee. You must also fill out and file the LLC corporate franchise tax form, which is included with the certificate of organization form.

California: Articles of organization in California must be filed with the California Secretary of State. There is no processing fee, however, there is a $15 handling fee for in-person submissions. Processing usually takes up to five business days. If you'd like a faster approval time, it is recommended to apply online, as they prioritize online submissions. You are still required to pay the annual $800 franchise tax fee.

Colorado: Articles of organization in Colorado must be filed with the Colorado Secretary of State online. There is a $50 filing fee. Colorado provides an LLC checklist to help you prepare what you need ahead of filing your articles of organization.

Connecticut: Certificates of organization in Connecticut must be filed with the Connecticut Secretary of State. There is a $120 filing fee that you must submit when filing your form. Processing can take up to six weeks, but if you'd like your application reviewed sooner, you can pay an additional fee of $50.

Delaware: A certificate of formation in Delaware must be filed with the Delaware Division of Corporations. You can either submit your form using its online document upload service or mail the request to their office. There is a $90 state filing fee. To speed up processing, you can also pay a $50 24-hour fee or a $100 same-day fee.

District of Columbia: Articles of organization in the District of Columbia must be filed with the D.C. Department of Licensing and Consumer Protection. There is a processing fee of $220 and it can take up to 15 business days for approval. You file your form online, by mail, or in person. Walk-in filings will be charged an expedited fee of $100 for the one-day service.

Florida: Articles of organization in Florida must be filed with the Florida Division of Corporations. There is a $125 processing fee, which includes the designation of the registered agent. The processing time in Florida is usually between 2 to 14 business days.

Georgia: Articles of organization in Georgia must be filed with the Georgia Secretary of State. You can submit your form online or by mail. There is a $100 filing fee when filing online, and an extra $10 paper filing fee when submitting your application by mail or in person. Processing time can take up to 15 days, but you may pay an additional $100 fee for faster processing.

Hawaii: Articles of organization in Hawaii must be filed with the Hawaii Department of Commerce and Consumer Affairs Business Registration Division. The filing fee is $50 with an additional filing fee of $25 if you'd like to expedite the filing process. Processing usually takes three to five business days or one day for expedited filing.

Idaho: A certificate of organization in Idaho must be filed with the Idaho Secretary of State. There is a $100 filing fee with an additional $20 added on if you're submitting a non-electronic form. You can pay an additional $40 for expedited processing or $100 for same-day services. Processing time can take seven to 10 business days, or more when filing by mail.

Illinois: Certificates of organization in Illinois must be filed with the Illinois Secretary of State. There is a $150 filing fee, and an additional $100 expedited fee if you need approval faster. Processing time can take up to 10 days.

Indiana: Articles of organization in Indiana must be filed with the Indiana Secretary of State Business Services Division using this form. There is a $90 filing fee, and processing times may vary depending on the method of submission.

Iowa: Certificates of organizations in Iowa must be filed with the Iowa Secretary of State. There is no official form, but the state provides an overview of what's needed on the document. There is a $50 fee that can be paid when submitting your document online or by mail.

Kansas: Articles of organization in Kansas must be filed with the Kansas Secretary of State. There is a $165 filing fee for paper forms and a $160 filing fee when submitting your application online. Processing typically takes two to three business days but may be faster with online filing.

Kentucky: Articles of organization in Kentucky must be filed with the Kentucky Secretary of State. There is a $40 filing fee, and documents are usually processed the same day but can take up to three business days.

Louisiana: Articles of organization in Louisiana must be filed with the Louisiana Secretary of State. There is a $100 filing fee and an additional $30 24-hour expediting fee, or a $50 same-day fee if you'd like to bring the document into the office. Processing can take one to seven business days but may be faster when filing online.

Maine: A certificate of formation in Maine must be filed with the Maine Secretary of State. There is a $175 filing fee and processing can take 20 to 25 business days. However, you can pay an additional $100 same-day processing fee for immediate service or an additional $50 24-hour processing fee.

Maryland: Articles of organization in Maryland must be filed with the Maryland Department of Assessments and Taxation. There is a $100 filing fee and a $20 fee for the Certificate of Status at the time of filing. Processing can take four to six weeks, but an expediting fee of $50 is available if you'd like to have your documents processed within seven business days.

Massachusetts: A certificate of organization in Massachusetts must be filed with the Massachusetts secretary of the commonwealth. The filing fee is $500 and approval time can take one to two business days if you file online.

Michigan: Articles of organization in Michigan must be filed with the Michigan Corporation Divisions. The filing fee is $50, with additional fees added if you'd like 24-hour, same-day, or one to two-hour expedited processing. These fees range from $50 to $1,000 depending on the option you choose.

Minnesota: Articles of organization in Minnesota must be filed with the Minnesota Secretary of State. There is a $155 filing fee for expedited in-person and online filings and a $135 filing fee for mail-in applications. Processing typically takes three to five business days.

Mississippi: A certificate of formation in Mississippi must

be filed online with the Mississippi Secretary of State. There is a $50 filing fee, and processing usually takes one to two business days.

Missouri: Articles of organization in Missouri must be filed with the Missouri Secretary of State. The filing fee is $105 for paper documents or $50 for online filing, with an additional convenience fee. Processing times vary.

Montana: Articles of organization in Montana must be filed with the Montana Secretary of State. There is a $35 filing fee and an additional filing fee to register an assumed business name (or DBA) with the state.

Nebraska: Certificates of organization in Nebraska must be filed with the Nebraska Secretary of State. There is a $110 in-office filing fee and a $100 online filing fee. Processing can take one to two business days. In Nebraska, all owners of newly formed businesses must publish a notice of formation in one newspaper for three consecutive weeks once the articles are filed.

Nevada: Articles of organization in Nevada must be filed with the Nevada Secretary of State. Documents are usually processed the same day when filing online. There is a $75 filing fee, with 24-hour, 2-hour, and one-hour expedited options available for an additional fee.

New Hampshire: Certificates of formation in New Hampshire must be filed with the New Hampshire State Corporation Commission. The form must be legibly printed with black ink or typed on an 8.5" x 11" piece of paper and maintain 1" margins. Pencil or erasable ink isn't accepted. The filing fee is $100.

New Jersey: Certificates of formation in New Jersey must be filed with the state of New Jersey. There is a $125 filing fee. You must also file Form NJ-REG for tax/employer registration. Processing can take up to four weeks, but expedited options are available for an additional fee.

New Mexico: Articles of organization in New Mexico must be filed with the New Mexico Secretary of State. There is a $50 filing fee, and processing can take one to three business days.

New York: Articles of organization in New York must be filed with the New York State Division of Corporations. There is a $200 filing fee, and the documents will be processed within minutes when filing online. After your articles are approved, you'll be required to publish a notice in a newspaper.

North Carolina: Articles of organization in North Carolina must be filed with the North Carolina Secretary of State. There is a $125 filing fee, and processing can take three to five business days. Expedited processing is available for additional fees.

North Dakota: Articles of organization in North Dakota must be filed with the North Dakota Secretary of State. There is a $135 filing fee, and it can take up to four weeks for documents to be processed.

Ohio: Articles of organization in Ohio must be filed with the Ohio Secretary of State. There is a $99 filing fee, and processing usually takes three to seven business days. Faster processing times are available with an additional fee.

Oklahoma: Articles of organization in Oklahoma must be filed with the Oklahoma Secretary of State. There is a $100 filing fee, and processing time may vary.

Oregon: Articles of organization in Oregon must be filed with the Oregon Secretary of State. There is a $100 processing fee. Processing can take six to eight weeks for mail-in forms but may be faster when filing online or in person.

Pennsylvania: Certificates of organization in Pennsylvania must be filed with the Pennsylvania Department of State. There is a $125 filing fee, and processing can take up to 15 business days.

Rhode Island: Articles of organization in Rhode Island must be filed with the Rhode Island Secretary of State. The filing fee is $150, and processing can take as little as two days when filed online.

South Carolina: Articles of organization in South Carolina must be filed with the South Carolina Secretary of State. There is a $110 filing fee, and processing usually takes 24 hours for online filing and two to three business days when filing by mail.

South Dakota: Articles of organization in South Dakota must be filed with the South Dakota Secretary of State. There is a $165 filing fee when filing by paper or a $150 filing fee when filing online. Processing can take three to five business days, but expedited processing is available for an additional $50.

Tennessee: Articles of organization in Tennessee must be filed with the Tennessee Secretary of State. The filing fee is $50 per member, with a minimum fee of $300 and a maximum fee of $3,000. Processing times may vary but may be faster when filing online.

Texas: Certificates of formation in Texas must be filed with the Texas Secretary of State. There is a $300 filing fee.

Processing time can take 70 to 72 days for nonexpedited documents sent by mail or fax, 12 to 14 days for expedited documents sent by mail or fax, and 10 to 15 days when submitted online.

Utah: Certificates of organization in Utah must be filed with the Utah Department of Commerce, which must be typed and not handwritten. There is a $54 filing fee, and processing can take three to 10 business days.

Vermont: Articles of organization in Vermont must be filed with the Vermont Secretary of State. There is a $125 filing fee, and processing can take less than one business day when filing online, or seven to 10 business days when filing by mail.

Virginia: Articles of organization in Virginia must be filed with the Virginia State Corporation Commission. There is a $100 filing fee. and processing times are faster when filed online.

Washington: Certificates of formation in Washington must be filed with the Washington State Corporation Commission. The filing fee is $180, with an additional $50 fee if you'd like to expedite filing. Online and expedited filing is usually processed within two business days.

West Virginia: Articles of organization in West Virginia must be filed with the West Virginia State Corporation Commission. There is a $100 filing fee that can be waived if you have a veteran-owned business. Processing can take five to 10 business days, but expedited processing is available for an additional fee.

Wisconsin: Articles of organization in Wisconsin must be filed with the Wisconsin Department of Financial Institutions. There is a $175 filing fee and an additional

$25 fee if you'd like expedited processing. Processing generally takes up to five business days.

Wyoming: Articles of organization in Wyoming must be filed with the Wyoming Secretary of State. There is a $100 filing fee, and processing can take up to 15 business days. Expedited processing is not available.

LLC ARTICLES OF ORGANIZATION FAQ

Ready to start filing? Here are some important questions and answers to remember when completing your LLC articles of organization.

Do I need an attorney to file articles of organization?

An attorney is not required, and you can file articles of organization by yourself. Each state has different rules and regulations for filing, however. Thus, a business attorney may be able to help you navigate the process and help you better understand and prepare.

Do I need to register my business name?

If you are filing articles of organization, you don't need to register your business name. Registering your LLC in the articles of organization also serves as registering your business name.

What forms do I need to file articles of organization?

This depends on the state you're filing in. Some states will require other forms, such as a docketing statement or an initial list of managers or managing members. Check with your state to see if there are additional forms that are required. Or follow the state-by-state guide above for more information.

How do you write articles of organization?

Writing an articles of organization for an LLC is simple because most states have the form created and ready for you to fill out. This takes the hassle out of having to create it yourself.

All you'll need to do is download the form and fill in the information, like your LLC's name, address, type of business, the purpose of business, and more. Make sure you're downloading your state's correct form, as some states may require additional information.

Are articles of organization on public record?

Articles of organization are public records if they're filed with the state. If you're starting a company, ensure you don't reveal confidential information.

MAKING CHANGES TO AN LLC BY FILING ARTICLES OF AMENDMENT

Changing your LLCs formation documents is generally a simple and straightforward process.

Reasons for changing your articles of organization can be simple as needing to change your company name or more complicated. Whatever your reason, completing and filing a simple form with the state is usually all you need to do to amend an LLC's articles of operation.

ARTICLES OF AMENDMENT

To make any changes, the LLC must file articles of amendment—also sometimes called a certificate of amendment or a certificate of change—with the state.

The articles of amendment document is easy to prepare. Information typically required includes:

- the business name as it appears on the articles of organization
- the date of organization
- the information being changed, such as a new LLC name or a change of business address
- the exact text of the articles that the LLC is changing
- the name and address of the registered agent
- signature of the person authorized to sign off on all paperwork

Be sure to check with your state's filing office regarding the specific information and forms required.

Restated articles of organization

Once an LLC has filed articles of amendment to change its original articles of organization, it needs to file restated articles of organization to make additional changes to its articles of organization.

The restated articles of organization include both the changes made by the articles of amendment and the new changes.

LLC OPERATING AGREEMENT

An operating agreement defines the organizational structure of your company and sets up a chain of command. Although not every state requires one, it protects your interests when starting your business—even if you're forming a single-member LLC.

The purpose of an operating agreement is to define rules and guidelines for a business. As the business owner, your personal liability might increase without the structure laid out in an operating agreement. Even if your state doesn't require one, it might be wise to consider drafting an agreement to protect your interests.

For example, if your LLC has multiple members who each contributed different amounts when forming the business, you might want to stipulate a profit split reflecting those contributions. Without an operating agreement, your business is governed by the rules in your state, meaning you could be subject to an even split of all profits.

WHAT AN OPERATING AGREEMENT SHOULD INCLUDE

An operating agreement should outline voting rights, member responsibilities, and even meeting frequency. While many states do not require any particulars, it's wise to make an agreement that's specific to your needs.

These items can help you clearly explain each part of your business and prove its legitimacy, although your operating agreement will depend on the size of your LLC, your expansion plans, and more.

Name and address of your LLC

Include the legal name of the LLC and its registered address. Depending on your state, you might need to add the words "Limited Liability Company" or "LLC" to your company's official name. Most states require that your company's address must:

- Be able to receive mail
- Be permanent and not a P.O. box

LLC articles of organization

File articles of organization with the secretary of state in the state where your business is based. Include this document in your operating agreement to:

- Verify the business's legitimacy
- Prove the founding date

Purpose of your LLC

This is the intention of your company. What does your business hope to accomplish? You'll answer this question when writing your business purpose. A purpose statement usually includes:

- An overview of what the business does
- The state where the business operates

Once you file articles of organization with the secretary of state, you can move ahead with writing your operating agreement. The filing fee for the articles ranges from less than $100 to more than $500, depending on your state.

HOW TO GET AN OPERATING AGREEMENT

To get an operating agreement, you can write it yourself or hire help to write it for you. You'll file this document internally since it governs most of your organization from top to bottom. Make a checklist with these steps before drafting your agreement:

File articles of organization

Once you file articles of organization with the secretary of state, you can move ahead with writing your operating agreement. The filing fee ranges from less than $100 to more than $500, depending on your state.

Write the operating agreement

Follow the steps above to craft an operating agreement that addresses your LLC's exact needs. Once you've completed the operating agreement, you'll need to ensure member consensus.

Sign the document

Each member should sign the agreement to indicate the validity and help your operating agreement's credibility if it is ever questioned.

File the operating agreement securely

When filing your operating agreement, make copies and distribute them to any members. Nonmembers are not required to see the operating agreement.

OPERATING AGREEMENT FAQS

Don't get hung up on these common questions about LLC operating agreements.

Is an operating agreement required?

Not in every state. Five states require that LLCs operating agreements: California, Delaware, Missouri, New York, and Maine. Still, it's a good idea to maintain an operating agreement within your own files, regardless of which state you live in.

Is an LLC agreement the same as an operating agreement?

An LLC agreement could refer to an operating agreement or to articles of organization—LLC agreement is not a generally known entity.

What does an operating agreement cost?

Operating agreements do not cost money, since no state requires you to file an official copy. Instead, it's recommended that you hire a lawyer to help you craft this complex and crucial legal document. Depending on who you hire, the price of an operating agreement varies.

Can you amend an operating agreement?

Operating agreements can be amended, but the agreement itself might dictate how that amendment can come into effect. Amendments need member approval and subsequent documentation to make sure they're enforced. An operating agreement might require a certain majority of votes to pass an amendment.

REASONS TO FORM AN LLC

Limited Liability Companies (LLCs) are flexible — you can use them for practically any purpose — and they offer more benefits than any other entity type. They have a favorable pass-through tax status, and with the dual liability protection that LLCs offer, corporations and limited partnerships can't compare. Following are some good reasons to form an LLC.

To customize your small business

LLCs are great for small businesses because they're adaptable to all situations. No matter whether you have 100 silent investors or are a two-person small-business operation, the LLC is so flexible that you can pretty much write the operating agreement to suit your needs; you can make your own rules and tailor your entity to suit the intricacies of your business.

To protect real estate assets

The LLC is a perfect entity for real estate holdings — you just can't beat it! One advantage is that an LLC has dual liability protection that shields your investments from the frivolous lawsuits filed against people like you every day. So if you rear-end someone in a parking lot and he sues you personally, he can't seize and liquidate your investment properties to settle the claim if they're held in an LLC.

To shield intellectual property

Unless you have a bunch of important patents, placing all your intellectual property in separate LLCs is overkill. You don't want your intellectual property to operate with the public; that's your operating company's job. So how do you link your intellectual property in your LLC to your operating company?

To raise seed capital for your business

The LLC is quickly becoming the entity of choice for raising seed or angel capital — early-stage investments under $500,000 or so. Whereas venture capital firms generally prefer to invest in corporations because they're most familiar with them, smaller investors love limited liability companies.

To plan your estate

Don't overlook the value of the LLC when you plan your estate. Although it's a simple entity in comparison to some of the über-complex trusts that your attorney may recommend, the LLC provides powerful asset protection. LLCs protect you not only from creditors, but also from probate lawyers and court costs.

They allow you to avoid probate altogether, which means that your estate isn't subject to the nickel-and-diming that probate attorneys siphon from estates as the court divvies up assets.

To do a short-term project

LLCs were made for short-term projects. When these entities were first introduced, they were never supposed to live forever like corporations do. That's why, when you create your articles of incorporation, you state a specific dissolution date or term, the number of years that the LLC is to be in existence.

To segregate assets

Segregating assets is vital in business. By segregating your business assets into individual LLCs, you put them out of the reach of your company's creditors or people who may want to sue you.

A lot of people incorrectly think that if they're operating as a corporation or an LLC, then their assets are safe, but that's not necessarily true. If you're like most entrepreneurs, your business is your biggest asset. If you lose the ability to operate, you're doomed.

Your business may be protected from your personal creditors, and you may be protected from your business's creditors; however, what protects your business from its own creditors? If your LLC gets sued, everything inside it can be seized and liquidated. Even worse, the courts can put a lien on your company and then do an asset freeze, which means that you have zero access to your operating capital — you can't write checks or receive funds from clients.

To minimize your tax burden

When you first go into business, chances are your company won't be profitable right away. Building up a business takes time, and in the first year or two, you probably will incur thousands of dollars in losses. A lot of entrepreneurs, eager to soften the financial blow of the startup phase, decide to form an LLC.

With an LLC and its default partnership taxation, the losses of the business flow through to the members so that they can use them as deductions for other income.

To change the profit distributions

An LLC's profits can be paid out disproportionately to the actual ownership percentages, so you and your partners can set up the company so that you receive all the profits and losses — even if you own only 10 percent of the company.

Why would you want to do that? Well, a common reason for changing the distributions is to provide an extra incentive for investors. For example, if one investor contributes all the capital, he gets 50 percent of the company.

However, the profit distributions can be varied so that he receives 100 percent of the profits until his investment has been paid back (plus 10 percent in some cases). Then the profit distributions return to normal, and the profit is split equitably among the members.

To protect your personal assets

When you spend your entire life saving for retirement, your children's education, or even that second home you've long dreamed about, nothing is more crippling than losing it all in a lawsuit. If you're like most people, you currently hold all your personal assets in your own name: your savings account, your cars, and your mutual funds, stocks, and bonds.

FREQUENTLY ASKED QUESTIONS ABOUT LLCS

Should I Form an LLC?

Forming an LLC offers major benefits for most small to medium business owners. Registering and operating as an LLC will provide business owners legal protection for personal assets, credibility and a long list of other advantages usually only found spread throughout a number of other business structures.

What is a foreign limited liability company?

A foreign LLC simply refers to one that operates in a different state than the one it was formed in. This is especially common for businesses located in cities close to state lines, where they may want to expand across the border. Operating in multiple states may make the LLC obligated to register documentation, pay taxes, and obtain other licenses in each state. And since each state has its own laws for governing LLCs, the business must make sure they stay in compliance with all of them.

Do I need to hire a lawyer to register an LLC?

No. Filing and registering an LLC with any given state does

not require an attorney. For more complicated business structures and those who want to ensure no mistakes are made, hiring a lawyer may be advisable. Generally, however, forming an LLC does not specifically require hiring a lawyer. If you do want legal assistance at an affordable rate, consider using one of the best LLC services.

Is an LLC the same thing as a corporation?

An LLC offers some benefits of a corporation and vice versa, but an LLC and a corporation are two different business entities and are not the same thing. Learn more about LLCs vs corporations to determine which structure is best for your business.

What kind of tax flexibility does an LLC provide?

LLCs can be taxed as sole proprietorships, partnerships, C corporations or S corporations. This choice allows members of an LLC to minimize their tax burden.

Is it possible to set up an LLC for free?

While the cost to register an LLC varies by state, there is a fee to register in every state. So, while there are some companies that advertise "free" LLC formation, what this really means is that the company will fill out the LLC paperwork for you for free. But again, you will still be responsible for the state's filing fee.

Is an LLC different from having liability insurance?

An LLC is not a commercial liability insurance policy and does not offer the same benefits. While an LLC protects you from personal liability from most business debts, liability insurance can protect you in the event someone claims your business caused an injury or property damage. Liability insurance for a business is also advisable in addition to the legal protections personal assets may receive from an LLC business structure.

STEPS TO SETTING UP A LIMITED LIABILITY COMPANY (LLC)

The limited liability company (LLC) has in recent years become the most popular legal structure for small businesses seeking personal liability protection and flexibility. The exact requirements vary slightly from state to state, but setting up an LLC is a relatively simple process that can usually be done in one to four hours, depending on the complexity of your organizational structure.

Regardless of the state you live in, here are the basics.

OBTAIN A COPY OF YOUR STATE'S LLC ARTICLES OF ORGANIZATION FORM

You'll get this form online from your state's Secretary of State website or office. When you contact them, also find out if the state (or county) in which you are setting up requires you to post a notice in the newspaper. Also, find out any specific rules regarding business names.

CHOOSE A NAME FOR YOUR BUSINESS

When setting up an LLC, you'll need to choose a business name that complies with your state's rules for LLC names. The main part of the business name is generally very flexible, but each state has a list of prohibited words, such as "corporation," "incorporated," "insurance," "city," and others. Your legal name must end with an LLC designator, such as "Limited Liability Company," "LLC," etc. Also, the name cannot be the same as another LLC on file in the state in which you are filing.

FILL OUT THE LLC ARTICLES OF ORGANIZATION FORM

This is usually a relatively simple process, as the only things you need to notify the state about regarding your LLC are items such as name, its business purpose, principal office address, the registered agent for receiving any legal documents, and the names of the initial members. You do not have to specify at this point the ownership distribution or management structure, just the names of the LLC's members.

PUBLISH A NOTICE IN YOUR LOCAL NEWSPAPER

Depending upon the requirements for your state and county when setting up an LLC, you may be required to publish a notice in a local newspaper stating your intention to form an LLC (if required by your state—don't waste the money otherwise). This should be done prior to filing your Articles of Organization. Currently, this step is only required in Nebraska, Arizona, and New York. Check with your state's Secretary of Stateto be certain.

SUBMIT YOUR ARTICLES OF ORGANIZATION FORM

You'll send this document to your Secretary of State along with the appropriate filing fee when setting up an LLC. Be careful: some states may have a corporate tax that is separate from the filing fee but which must be paid at the time of filing. For example, California has only a $70 filing fee, but an $800 annual tax.

THE LLC OPERATING AGREEMENT

While you're done in terms of legal requirements, there's still a very important piece missing: the LLC operating agreement. However, the operating agreement is not always required by the state and can be created after the legal filings are done. If you are the sole owner of the LLC, you probably don't need one at this point. However, if there's even just one other owner, it's best to make a written agreement of the terms.

Create an LLC Operating Agreement

Make sure your operating agreement spells out the financial and management rights and responsibilities of the LLC members, such as: who contributes what if the LLC needs additional capital, when and how profits from the business will be distributed, under what terms members can leave the LLC, etc. Even (or perhaps especially) among friends and family, leaving these questions unanswered can create strains on both the business and personal relationships down the road. Put it in writing.

GET ON THE SAME PAGE WITH YOUR BUSINESS PARTNERS

Although not legally required, you should probably work out the details of the operating agreement well in advance of filing the LLC articles of organization. You may find that one of your potential business partners doesn't want to be a part of it once they know the whole deal, or perhaps that you need to bring in someone else. Work it out in advance.

DO IT YOURSELF

You can hire an attorney or turn to popular websites like LegalZoom for helping you through the process of setting up an LLC, but really, unless your organization is fairly complex, you can do this yourself and save a whole lot of money—which just became a very important resource for your new business.

SET UP YOUR LLC IN THE STATE YOU'RE DOING BUSINESS

Unless you have a compelling reason otherwise, it's generally best for small businesses to set up in the state in which it will principally be doing business. There are some tax and organizational advantages to registering in certain states, however. Delaware, Nevada, and Wyoming are popular for out-of-state registration, but before making that decision, consult with an attorney and research it further if you're in doubt. Typically, in order to see significant advantages in setting up your LLC in one of these tax-friendly states, you'll need to be generating a large amount of income. It's wise to set up your LLC where you live today and consider switching once you're bringing in a lot of revenue.

HOW TO PAY YOURSELF IN AN LLC

Forming a limited liability company, or LLC, can be a great way to organize your company and protect yourself from liability. However, you still need to earn a living, so you may be wondering, "How to pay myself from my LLC?"

The two most common options are to treat yourself as an employee with wages, or to treat yourself as an LLC member and receive distribution from the profits.

Paying yourself from an LLC as an employee allows you to receive regular compensation that you can plan on throughout the year, which can be very helpful if you are seeking a regular income.

Where there are multiple owners, if all of the LLC members participate equally in the operation of the business, you can't pay one a salary and not the others. However, if you are the only member that has a management role, you can pay yourself a salary without setting up salaries for the other participating LLC members.

Employee wages are considered operating expenses for the LLC and will be deducted from the LLC's profits. The Internal Revenue Service (IRS) only allows reasonable wages as a deduction, so be sure any salary you pay yourself is within industry norms. You can also issue bonuses to LLC members who are employees, including yourself. Again, these must be reasonable related to the salary being paid.

You'll need to file IRS Form W-4 to determine the amount of payroll withholding from each paycheck you receive. The LLC will pay you as a W-2 employee and will withhold income and employment taxes from your paycheck. You will pay income tax on your wages earned.

Receive distributions from LLC profits

Another option for how to pay yourself in an LLC is to receive distributions of profits from the LLC each year. Each member owns a percentage of the LLC, called his or her capital account. Year-end profit distributions are made based on that percentage. So if the LLC had $100,000 in profit and you and the other member each own 50%, you can each receive $50,000.

You also could set up a draw to receive ongoing payments as a draw against the year-end profit. If you expect your percentage of the year-end profit to be $12,000, you could set up a draw to receive $1,000 each month. The total of all the draws throughout the year are deducted from the total year-end profit. So if your draw for the year totaled $12,000, but your share of the profit ends up being $15,000, then you would receive $3,000 at the end of the year.

If you are the only member of the LLC, you will pay income tax on your distributions and you will file Schedule C to report the profits and losses of the LLC with your personal tax return. If there is more than one member, the IRS treats the LLC as a partnership and you each report your share of the profit and pay income tax on that. The LLC will file IRS Form 1065 to report how profits are divided among the members.

It's important to note that receiving a salary and receiving year-end distributions are not mutually exclusive. If you get a paycheck, you're still a member of the LLC and entitled to your year-end distribution.

Work as an independent contractor

A third option for paying yourself is to hire yourself as an independent contractor, doing work for the LLC you also own.

Here is an example: If you are a member of an LLC that prints signs, you can hire yourself as an independent contractor to do the graphic design for the signs. This type of arrangement may not offer as many benefits, though.

If you choose to pay yourself as a contractor, you need to file IRS Form W-9 with the LLC and the LLC will file an IRS Form 1099-MISC at the end of the year. You will be responsible for paying self-employment taxes on the amount earned.

Choose not to receive payments

You also have the option to not pay yourself anything and to leave the profits in the LLC. You still will need to pay income tax on the profit earned, since the profits from your LLC pass through to your personal tax return.

COMMON LLC CREATION MISTAKES

Starting a new business is exciting but also a little intimidating. There's a lot you probably don't know, and mistakes can end up costing you.

If you've decided to start a limited liability company (LLC), then you've already avoided the biggest mistake, which is not having a business entity at all. But you'll also want to avoid these 6 other common mistakes people make when starting an LLC.

Mistake 1: Choosing to Become an LLC When It's Not the Right Entity for Your Business

The first mistake people make when creating an LLC is choosing an LLC to begin with. The limited liability company is a great business structure for many business ventures, but it's not suitable for all.

The main consideration is money. Do you plan on growing with capital from outside investors? If so, a corporation is likely a better choice for you. Investors are typically more comfortable investing in corporations than in LLCs. Corporations are also the only entities that can issue stock, so if you dream of a big IPO in the future, then the corporation is the entity for you.

Mistake 2: Incorporating Your Business in the Wrong State

Once you've determined that the LLC is the right entity for your business, your next step is to decide on where to incorporate it, i.e., where to register it.

Most of the time, incorporating in the state where you live and do business is the best solution. Some entrepreneurs want to incorporate in other states like Delaware, Wyoming, or Nevada for the supposed tax and legal benefits. This can make sense for larger companies, but it rarely makes sense for smaller LLCs.

Incorporating your business in a state your business isn't based in means taking on hassles like maintaining a registered agent in both the state you live in and incorporate in, filing paperwork in both states, and paying fees to both states. After considering the time and money involved, it's typically not a savvy move for most LLCs. It's usually smarter to incorporate in your home state.

Mistake 3: Choosing the Wrong Type of LLC

There are actually four types of LLCs you can create in South Carolina, as we've covered before in a previous blog. Check out that blog for more information, but in short, know that an LLC can be either "term" or "at will" and "member managed" or "manager managed." If you select the wrong type when setting up your LLC, it can be bad for the LLC and the members down the line.

Mistake 4: Choosing a Bad Name

What makes a "bad" name? One that's already being used.

Before choosing a business name, do some research. You can search for existing business names in South Carolina here under "Existing Business," which is a good start. (South Carolina does not allow a new business to register a name that's not "grammatically distinguishable" from existing names.) You might also want to search the trademark database at the US Patent and Trademark Office here to see if the name you have in mind is being used somewhere else. Finally, a thorough Google search for your proposed name can turn up other uses of the name.

Your name matters because if you inadvertently violate someone else's trademark, you can get in trouble. Disputes over names can end up being costly and time-consuming if someone sues you over the name and you want to defend your right to use it. But even if you decide to let go of the name, it will cost you time and money to rebrand your digital and physical presence. Worse, you will have lost the brand recognition and goodwill you've built up over the years in your community. So choose wisely.

Mistake 5: Not Having Corporate Governance Documents

This is probably the single biggest mistake you can make when you plan to start an LLC with business partners. Many people go into business with friends or family members, and at the start everything is copacetic. Everyone gets along and there are no major disagreements. But many an experienced business attorney will tell you that times change, and that's when things can get ugly.

Imagine that you're in a business with two friends and everything is going well at first. Then one friend unexpectedly dies, and you find you're now in business with their spouse. Or the other friend starts slacking off, working fewer hours but taking the same profits as the hard-working partners. Or you become incapacitated and can no longer work. Or the three of you disagree on how to raise money for the company. What happens to you, your investment, and the business in these situations?

Corporate governance documents are intended to lay out the rules so that when a disagreement or unpleasant situation arises, what happens next is clear. These simple documents can preserve good relations between partners, protect the partners' investments, and protect the business itself.

Two important documents that any business owner with partners should consider getting during the creation of their business:

- An operating agreement. This spells out how the company should be managed, how profits and losses are handled, how much of the company each member owns, what each member's responsibilities are, and more.
- A buy-sell agreement. This document covers what happens to the business when a member dies, becomes incapacitated, stops working, etc. Read more about buy-sell agreements here.

By addressing future scenarios now, you can avoid major problems down the line. Just know that it's vital to discuss these things before you and your partners start operating your business.

Mistake 6: Not Getting Legal Assistance When You Need It

It's very easy to go online and get the forms to start an LLC yourself, without the help of an attorney. Is that smart?

In some cases, doing so is fine and poses no future problems, particularly with single-member LLCs that operate within one state and are wholly self-funded. These business owners would likely benefit from speaking with a business attorney, but they may feel pretty confident that they can create their LLC on their own.

But other entrepreneurs should consider speaking with an attorney before and during the creation process of their LLC. This is especially true in any of the following situations:

- You have business partners
- You plan to take on money from outside investors
- You plan to do business in multiple states

The cost is usually the main reason that people don't want to spend the money on an attorney at this stage, and that's understandable. Business owners want to make money before they spend it. But the money you spend up front on corporate governance documents or advice from an experienced attorney can save you money and mistakes down the road. (Plus, don't forget this expense is a business write-off when it comes to tax time.)

HOW TO CONVERT FROM A C CORP STRUCTURE TO AN LLC

C corporation (C corp) is a widely-used business structure in the U.S. following the numerous benefits to the owner and the organization as a whole. Despite its advantages, a few disadvantages of being a C corporation might lead the owner to convert it into a Limited Liability Company (LLC).

The decision to convert may come from various reasons. It could be to lower your tax burden or upgrade protection for liability and personal assets, or you simply want to reduce the paperwork you must do.

To guarantee a quick and efficient conversion process with the least stress, make sure you review your business's current status and each state's requirements before starting the conversion.

WAYS TO CONVERT A C CORPORATION TO AN LLC

If you're heading toward a change from a C corporation to an LLC, below are the three common ways to do it. Please be mindful that not all of these choices are approved in every state of the U.S.

Dissolving the corporation and forming a new LLC

This traditional method consists of two key steps: dissolving the C corporation and forming a new LLC. This process takes the longest to complete and might be subject to additional fees.

Generally, you will be going through:

- Step 1: Form a new LLC
- Step 2: Transfer assets and liabilities
- Step 3: Exchange for LLC memberships
- Step 4: Dissolve the corporation

There are exceptions, however. You can modify the process as required according to the current state of your corporation. Suppose that your corporation has no assets, forming the LLC and dissolving the C corp can happen simultaneously.

This may be the only option for states that don't allow conversion. Also, if your corporation has significant operating losses or heavily depreciated assets, your state authority may not allow you to merge or directly convert to an LLC.

MERGING OF THE CORPORATION WITH THE NEW LLC

Many states (e.g. Delaware, California, Texas, etc.) permit merging methods and impose specific requirements for this process. You'll be asked to engage in a "statutory merger", which involves creating a new LLC and merging the former corporation into that new entity.

The process will be consisting of the following steps:

- Step 1: Establish a new LLC
- Step 2: Prepare a merger agreement or plan
- Step 3: Obtain C corp's stockholders' and LLC's members' consent to the merger
- Step 4: Exchange shares of stock for LLC's membership interests
- Step 5: File a certificate of merger with the Secretary of State
- Step 6: Dissolve the C corp after merging

This process is more complicated and costly compared to the direct conversion method, which we'll discuss in detail below. For instance, the New York business corporation law and New York LLC law strictly regulate the merging of corporations into LLCs in New York.

Converting from a C Corporation into an LLC (limited to several states)

Statutory conversions are considered relatively new in the US. This allows you to convert a corporation to LLC directly instead of forming a new entity. To ensure a smooth transition, make sure you have the following in place:

- Have the current directors approve the conversion plan
- Conduct a meeting to request stockholders' approval on the conversion
- File with the secretary of state's office and pay the fees if any

WHY SHOULD YOU CONVERT A C CORP INTO AN LLC

Situation 1: You run a small business and aim for an informal ownership structure

An LLC can have unlimited owners with no restrictions on classification or nationality. You also don't have to take care of extensive paperwork and formalities. If you don't require a formal corporate structure of a C Corp and would prefer to manage your business with more flexibility, then converting to an LLC may be beneficial for your company.

Situation 2: You want to take advantage of certain tax benefits

Converting a C corp into an LLC can potentially help you gain access to certain tax benefits.

LLCs are usually taxed more favorably than C Corps since their profits and losses can be passed through to the owners and members of the LLC, so they do not have to pay corporate taxes. This can help to reduce the overall amount you have to pay.

LLCs typically benefit from pass-through taxation so as not to pay taxes at the business entity level, unless you file a Form 8832 and affirmatively elect to be treated as a corporation.

Situation 3: You would like more control over management decisions

LLCs provide their members with more control over the management decisions of the business, as members typically have the right to make day-to-day decisions without consulting with other owners.

This can be advantageous if you want more autonomy over operations and don't need a board or shareholders to approve of essential decisions like a C corp.

Situation 4: You want to be independent of investors

If you convert from a C corp to an LLC, you will be free from investors' or shareholders' oversight and potential interference.

In a C corp, investors may have a say in major decisions and can influence the direction of your business. Converting to an LLC will limit their influence, allowing you to remain independent while still having access to capital.

If any of these situations apply to you and your business, then converting from a C Corp to an LLC may be the right choice for you. Before making any decisions, it is best to consult with legal or tax professionals as they can provide customized advice on what structure is best for your company.

POTENTIAL CONSEQUENCES WHEN CONVERTING INTO AN LLC

When converting from a C Corporation to an LLC, you must be aware of the possible consequences that may arise.

Conversion cost & changes in tax structure

It is also important to keep in mind that the conversion process may come with added costs, depending on the state you are operating in. Additionally, the tax structure of your business may change when converting to an LLC.

Limited investment option

LLCs tend to provide limited investment options for members, as the structure does not offer shares that can be bought and sold on the public market. This means that you may not be able to raise capital as easily as you could with a C corp structure.

Risks of freedom granted in LLC

Finally, it is also important to consider that the freedom granted with an LLC structure may come with some risks. Since members have more autonomy over the business, they may also be more exposed to liabilities.

For instance, members may not be required to hold regular meetings or keep minutes, which could lead to mismanagement and at times legal disputes with creditors or investors.

HOW TO DISSOLVE AN LLC

Closing your business can be a long, involved process. You need to take the proper time to wrap up all your affairs in a neat little bow. Following the proper procedures can shield you from any potential liabilities and help you to move forward in your new endeavors as quickly as possible. Whatever the reason, here's how to dissolve an LLC to ensure you get it right.

Deciding to dissolve is the first step to closing a business. After that, you'll need to do several things to get things moving, including giving notice to your creditors, filing final tax returns and notifying any applicable government agencies.

Vote to Dissolve the LLC

Members who decide to dissolve the company are taking part in something called a voluntary dissolution. To do so, all members need to cast a vote or follow the guidelines for events that automatically trigger a dissolution, such as the death of a business partner. Reference your LLC operating agreement for the proper procedures. If your operating agreement doesn't address dissolution, follow the procedures outlined in your state's LLC laws.

Once everyone has voted and a majority agrees (or a

dissolution trigger has occurred), record the decision to dissolve the LLC and keep it with the company's official records.

File Your Final Tax Return

Some states require you to get a tax clearance or a verification of good standing from your state tax agency before you're allowed to file dissolution paperwork. Filing your tax returns and paying any taxes you may owe will satisfy this requirement.

When filing tax returns for your company, make sure to indicate somewhere that this will be your business' final tax return. You'll receive a clearance in the form of a certificate or letter from the tax agency stating you don't have any more tax liability.

Even if your state doesn't require a tax clearance, you'll still need to file final tax returns at both the state and federal level. You also need to file final employment tax returns–otherwise, you could be held personally liable for unpaid payroll taxes.

File an Article of Dissolution

Articles of dissolution is a document in which you ask the state to officially dissolve your business. Find the form at your state's corporations division or Secretary of State website. In some cases, the form may be called a certificate of dissolution or certificate of cancellation.

The form typically requires you to provide details about your company and its members. You may also be required to indicate if and when any assets have been distributed and whether any liabilities have been paid pack.

Most states charge a fee to file articles of dissolution, so make sure to include the correct amount.

Once approved, the state will send you a certificate of dissolution — keep this important document in your records.

Settle Outstanding Debts

Your state may require you to notify creditors before filing articles of dissolution. Creditors might include lenders, insurance carriers, service providers and suppliers. Some states also require dissolving LLCs to publish a notice in their local newspaper.

Your notice to creditors should give creditors a deadline for submitting claims and tell them that claims submitted after the deadline will be barred. Your state's laws will specify the appropriate deadline, but it's usually between 90 and 180 days.

Even if a notice to creditors isn't required, it's a good idea to send one. This allows you to pay all your obligations and reduces the chance you'll have liabilities unexpectedly surface in the future.

Distribute Assets

Once you've paid your taxes and your creditors, any remaining assets — including any investments, profits and tangible goods — can be distributed to the LLC's members. Your operating agreement (or state law, if you don't have one) will guide you on how to allocate assets among the members.

Conduct Other Wind Down Processes

Properly concluding your business includes letting go of employees, (and settling any severance packages, if applicable), paying final payroll taxes, negotiating cancellations of contracts and leases canceling business licenses and permits and letting customers know when your last date of business will be.

At the end of the process, you'll close your business bank accounts, Federal Employer Identification Number (FEIN) and state tax identification number if you have one.

HOW TO TRANSFER OWNERSHIP OF AN LLC

The process for transferring ownership of an LLC depends on the type of transfer as well as the provisions of your operating agreement.

One of the advantages of having a limited liability company (LLC) is that even when sold, the business may continue on as before with a simple transfer of ownership.

How to transfer ownership of an LLC is a topic that is generally covered extensively in the LLC's operating agreement. When forming an LLC, you likely signed an agreement that described how the business would function. Although this document is not required by law, most LLCs have them, and within them, you will find the exact process to follow when transferring ownership of your LLC.

Note that the process varies depending on whether the entire business is being sold or whether only the owner's names and percentage ownerships are changing.

What is a buy-sell agreement?

A buy-sell agreement is an agreement documented in the

operating agreement that outlines instructions for buying out a member of the LLC. Some specific issues covered include who may become an LLC member, whether the business must buy back shares from a departing member, the distribution of the remaining shares, and the process for approval of the transfer.

The agreement should also address how the business and membership interests in it will be valued in the case of interest transfer. This valuation method must be followed or the LLC could face a lawsuit by the departing member and stiff penalties for violating its own operating agreement.

BUYING OUT AN LLC MEMBER

While specific provisions vary, if the LLC is buying out a member's share, ownership transfer entails valuing the business and member shares to determine how much the departing member's share is worth. Usually, this departing member's share is then bought out by the LLC, and often, the transfer also must be approved by other LLC members.

If your operating agreement doesn't specify the change of ownership process, you must turn to your state's law for guidance. Some states require the complete dissolution of an LLC if an operating agreement doesn't provide for an ownership transfer process. Because this process can be detrimental to your business, you should consider this factor when forming the LLC to better lay a path for down the road even if you don't anticipate interest transfers.

SELLING AN LLC

Unlike the valuation of the business for buying out an LLC member, your operating agreement does not require a specific business valuation method or process for selling an LLC. In that sense, you are on your own to find a buyer and agree on a price. Your buyer may want to purchase the entire business or only its assets.

Once you have reached the terms of the sale, you can memorialize the terms in a preliminary memorandum or change of ownership letter. When both parties are satisfied, you can move forward with a formal transfer of business ownership agreement, which is executed just like any other type of contract according to your state's laws.

Because LLC transfers of ownership can have far-reaching and long-lasting consequences to a business, the best practice is to document the process as clearly as possible within the operating agreement at the formation of the LLC. Making sure you have LLC ownership transfer provisions in place from the beginning can save you major headaches later, which makes sound LLC legal advice a smart idea from the get-go.

HOW TO REMOVE A MEMBER FROM AN LLC

Removing a member from an LLC can be difficult, especially if the member doesn't want to go. Check your operating agreement and state laws to guide you through the process.

Many limited liability companies (LLCs) reach a point where the owners (or "members") can't or don't want to work together anymore. Usually, a member can leave an LLC voluntarily by following a few simple procedures. But involuntarily removing a member from an LLC can be complicated and contentious.

Here are general guidelines for removing an LLC member. The exact procedures you'll follow depend on your LLC's operating agreement and your state's LLC laws.

Follow Your Operating Agreement

An operating agreement is a blueprint for how your LLC will run, and it's usually created at the time an LLC is formed. Review your agreement to see whether it explains how to remove someone from your LLC. It may cover voluntary resignation, involuntary removals, or both. The agreement may explain the procedure for resigning, grounds for ousting a member, and the way removal must be voted on.

You'll also need to buy out the departing member's interest in the company. The operating agreement may explain how to do this. Owner buyouts may also be addressed in a separate document such as a buy/sell agreement.

If your operating agreement and other internal agreements cover your situation, follow the procedures outlined. Be sure to document your actions with resolutions, letters of resignation, valuations, or other appropriate documents and retain them in your company records.

Try to Negotiate a Deal

It's not unusual for operating agreements to be silent on the subject of involuntary member removals. Most LLC owners don't envision having to remove a partner from an LLC against the person's will. And even with a process in place, there's no guarantee the departing member will cooperate.

Since the next step likely involves going to court, it's worth trying to negotiate a deal to buy out the interest of the partner you want to remove. This may save you time and money in the long run. If you do reach a buyout agreement, be sure to put it in writing and follow your operating agreement's procedure for voluntary departures.

Refer to State LLC Law

When the operating agreement doesn't include a procedure for involuntary removal of a member and you can't reach an agreement, you'll need to turn to state law. Although state LLC laws vary, many are based on the

Revised Uniform Limited Liability Company Act.

Under this act, a court can involuntarily remove a member from an LLC for three reasons:

Misconduct that "adversely and materially" affects the company's business

Willful and persistent breach of the operating agreement or the person's duties as an LLC member or manager

That it's not reasonably practical to carry out the business with the person involved

Going to court to remove an LLC member can be a long, expensive, and emotionally draining process. In some states, your only option is to dissolve the LLC and form a new one if you want to continue in business. Before you file any legal action, get advice from a business lawyer who's familiar with your state's LLC laws.

After a Member Is Removed

If the removed member was an LLC officer or manager, you'll need to appoint someone new to carry out the former member's duties. If the member had authority to sign documents or conduct business on the LLC's behalf, notify financial institutions and others you do business with that the member is no longer affiliated with your company.

Check with your state to see whether you need to file any documents in light of the ownership change. And if your operating agreement doesn't adequately cover involuntary removal of a partner, consult a business lawyer about preparing a new operating agreement.

HOW TO ADD ANOTHER OWNER TO LLC

The process is straightforward, so long as you understand the consequences of adding an owner to your business.

Adding an owner to your limited liability company (LLC) isn't particularly difficult. But you need to follow the procedure outlined in your operating agreement or state law.

Remember, an LLC is a distinct business entity that protects its owners from personal liability. Following formal procedures and keeping good records helps to maintain that protection and to avoid future disputes among the owners.

Follow these steps for a smooth process when you add an owner to an LLC.

Understand the consequences

Before you add a new LLC member, you should fully consider both the benefits and the potential consequences. A new owner can contribute a great deal to an LLC but will also diminish the percentage of profits that go to the original owners. In a member-managed LLC, a new owner will also add another voice to the decision-making process. And once someone has an ownership interest, it may not be that easy to get rid of them if things don't work out as you expected.

Adding another owner can also have tax consequences. If you own a single-member LLC, you'll no longer have the option of being taxed as a sole proprietor—you will instead be taxed as a partnership or corporation.

To make sure you're fully aware of the impact of adding a new LLC member, it's wise to consult with a business attorney.

Review your operating agreement

Your LLC's operating agreement probably describes the procedure you must follow to add a new member, including the way the membership must be voted on. It is important to follow the procedure described in the agreement because it helps to show that your LLC really is an independent entity that follows its own rules.

If you don't have an operating agreement, or if your operating agreement doesn't discuss adding new members, you must follow the procedure described in your state's limited liability laws. In some states, you must dissolve and then re-form the LLC if there is any change in ownership.

If your LLC doesn't have an operating agreement, now is a good time to get one. An operating agreement is essential for multi-member LLCs because it spells out the rights and responsibilities of the owners and their respective shares of the business and its profits and losses. It is far easier and cheaper to draft an operating agreement than to try to resolve these issues when there's a dispute among the owners.

Decide on the specifics

Once you understand the procedure for adding a new owner, you must determine the specifics of your arrangement. LLCs are very flexible in their ownership structure: for example, a person can own a certain percentage of the business, but may be entitled to a different percentage of profits.

Discuss ownership percentages with the existing LLC members as well as the prospective new member to arrive at an agreement.

Prepare and vote on an amendment to add an owner to LLC

Once you have decided how to structure the new owner's interest, you should prepare an amendment to the operating agreement to add the new owner to the LLC. The amendment should list the new owner's name, any capital contribution that the new owner is making, the owner's percentage interest in the company, and the percentage of profits and losses that can be allocated to that owner.

The members should then formally vote on the amendment in the way described in the operating agreement. Document the vote in your LLC's minutes and/or with a resolution, and have all the LLC's members – including the new one – sign the amended operating agreement.

Keep the amended operating agreement at your place of business with your other important business documents.

Amend the articles of organization (if necessary)

When you formed the LLC, you filed articles of organization with the state. In some states, you may have to file a form amending the articles to add a new member.

In other states, there is no LLC member information in the articles, and no amendment is necessary.

You can check the requirements for your state by contacting the state agency responsible for business filings (usually this is the Secretary of State).

File any required tax forms

If you've been doing business as a single-member LLC and using your social security number as your federal tax identification number, you'll need to obtain a federal employer identification number (EIN) when you become a multi-member LLC. You can obtain an EIN for free by filling out a form on the IRS website.

If your LLC has been taxed as a sole proprietorship or partnership in the past and you now want to be taxed as a corporation, you'll need to file additional forms with the IRS to elect corporate status. A lawyer or tax accountant can advise you on the best tax status for your LLC.

Adding an LLC owner means taking on another business partner, so it's important to think things through before you act. Once you've made your decision, adding a new member is just a matter of following your operating agreement's procedures, creating a formal record of the new ownership, and filing any required documents with the state.